M000087913

Create & Take Bible Crafts

Parables and Miracles

For information regarding the CPSIA on this printed material call:
203-595-3636 and provide reference # LANC-315751

These pages may be copied.
Permission is granted to the original buyer of this book to
photocopy student materials in this book for use
with pupils in Sunday school or Bible teaching classes.

Rainbow Publishers®
www.RainbowPublishers.com

Create & Take Bible Crafts

Parables and Miracles

Enelle Eder

This book is dedicated to my Dad, Rev. James Pulham, who has spent the best part of his life sharing these same stories and truths with his congregation. Thank you for the solid foundation you gave me to grow on.

CREATE & TAKE BIBLE CRAFTS: PARABLES AND MIRACLES
©2011 by Rainbow Publishers, ninth printing
ISBN 10: 1-58411-007-4
ISBN 13: 978-1-58411-007-1
Rainbow reorder# RB38021
RELIGION / Christian Ministry / Children

Rainbow Publishers
P.O. Box 261129
San Diego, CA 92196
www.RainbowPublishers.com

Interior Illustrator: Chuck Galey
Cover Illustrator: Robin Olimb

Scriptures are from the *Holy Bible*: New International Version (North American Edition), ©1973, 1978, 1984 by the International Bible Society. Used by permission of Zondervan Bible Publishers.

Permission is granted to the buyer of this book to photocopy student materials for use with Sunday school or Bible teaching classes.

All rights reserved. Except as noted above, no part of this publication may be reproduced, stored in a retrieval system, or transmitted in any form or by any means without written permission of Rainbow Publishers.

Printed in the United States of America

Table of Contents

Create • Take • Create • Take • Create • Take • Create • Take • Create

Create & Take
Memory Verses

To Families

We have some exciting crafts planned for use in teaching Bible lessons. We would like to ask your help in saving or collecting the following checked items.

❏ buttons
❏ chenille wire
❏ clear, self-stick plastic
❏ clothespins
❏ construction paper
❏ craft foam
❏ craft glue
❏ craft sticks
❏ crepe paper streamers
❏ dish soap bottles
❏ egg shells
❏ felt
❏ foam meat trays
❏ foam plates
❏ gift wrap tubes
❏ hole punch
❏ magnets

❏ ornament hooks
❏ pearls
❏ pebbles
❏ plastic covers
❏ plastic cups
❏ plastic drinking straws
❏ plastic juice jars
❏ plastic spoons and forks
❏ pom-poms
❏ poster board
❏ pot pie pans
❏ powdered fruit drink containers
❏ red ribbon
❏ resealable plastic sandwich bags
❏ sand

❏ seeds
❏ sequins
❏ small milk cartons
❏ soil
❏ sponges
❏ tempera paint
❏ toilet tissue rolls
❏ toothpicks
❏ transparency sheets
❏ vegetable net bags
❏ wiggle eyes
❏ wooden beads
❏ yarn
❏ yellow Easter grass

Please bring in the items on _____

Thank you for your help!

To Families

We have some exciting crafts planned for use in teaching Bible lessons. We would like to ask your help in saving or collecting the following checked items.

❏ buttons
❏ chenille wire
❏ clear, self-stick plastic
❏ clothespins
❏ construction paper
❏ craft foam
❏ craft glue
❏ craft sticks
❏ crepe paper streamers
❏ dish soap bottles
❏ egg shells
❏ felt
❏ foam meat trays
❏ foam plates
❏ gift wrap tubes
❏ hole punch

❏ magnets
❏ ornament hooks
❏ pearls
❏ pebbles
❏ plastic covers
❏ plastic cups
❏ plastic drinking straws
❏ plastic juice jars
❏ plastic spoons and forks
❏ pom-poms
❏ poster board
❏ pot pie pans
❏ powdered fruit drink containers
❏ red ribbon
❏ resealable plastic sandwich bags

❏ sand
❏ seeds
❏ sequins
❏ small milk cartons
❏ soil
❏ sponges
❏ tempera paint
❏ toilet tissue rolls
❏ toothpicks
❏ transparency sheets
❏ vegetable net bags
❏ wiggle eyes
❏ wooden beads
❏ yarn
❏ yellow Easter grass

Please bring in the items on _____

Thank you for your help!

Introduction

All children love crafts! However, in today's fast-paced world, a simple coloring project is no longer adequate to hold a child's attention. *Create & Take Bible Crafts* is a set of five books that gives you new ideas for teaching important eternal truths. These activities are designed to help you teach your children about God through Bible-based lessons.

Each of the five books contains over 25 different topics to discuss and unique crafts to accompany them. A memory verse, which relates directly to the topic, is provided for each lesson. Encourage the children to write the memory verse on the craft whenever possible as a take-home reminder.

Detailed instructions and full-size, reproducible patterns are included for each craft. And they can be made from household materials or basic craft supplies. A list of supplies is provided on page 7 in a reproducible note format so you can ask for families' assistance in collecting materials.

Each lesson is labeled according to the age appropriateness based on the subject matter and difficulty of the craft. However, use your own judgment as to which lessons and crafts are suitable for the skills and interests of your students. You will find that the lessons can be successfully adapted for use in Sunday school, children's church, vacation Bible school, Christian school or wherever God's Word is taught.

With *Create & Take Bible Crafts* your children will not only create and take crafts — they will make new commitments that will take them into a life of serving the Lord.

The Centurion

Ages 8-11

Memory Verse

Go! It will be done just as you believed.

~Matthew 8:13

....

Faith

When Jesus was teaching in Capernaum, a centurion soldier of great authority came to see Him. "Authority" means he had official power.

The man asked Jesus to heal his servant, who was sick at home. Jesus said He would go to the man's house and heal him.

But the soldier told Him, "I do not deserve to have You come to my house. I know that You can just say the word here and he will be well."

Then he told Jesus that he himself was a man of authority because whatever he commanded of the soldiers serving under him, they would do. Recognizing Jesus' great authority, the soldier knew Jesus could command the servant to be healed and it would happen.

Jesus was so amazed by the man's faith that He told him to go on his way and the healing would be done.

Do you have enough faith in Jesus' authority to ask Him for something and then go your way believing it is done? If we know that God is in control of everything, we should have the same kind of faith that the centurion soldier had.

— based on Matthew 8:5-13

For Discussion

1. What does authority mean?

2. What did the centurion want Jesus to do?

3. How much faith did the centurion have?

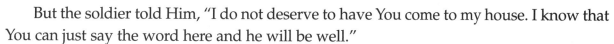

Create • Take • Create • Take • Create • Take • Create • Take • Create

A Sword of Faith

What You Need

- gift wrap tube
- construction paper
- markers
- scissors
- glue
- stapler
- cottage cheese container lids

Before Class

Cut 18" from a gift wrap tube, one per child. Throw away the other ends. Cut a sheet of black construction paper into an 18" x 6" rectangle, one per child.

What to Do

1. Show the children how to cut four 1½" slits down one end of the tube, spacing the slits evenly.

2. Show how to pinch two opposite tabs of the tube into a fold and bend them toward the center of the tube. Have the students staple these to secure them.

3. Show how to push the other two tabs flat against the stapled tabs and staple again. Allow the students to trim the edges so that the sword comes to a flat point.

4. Have the students cover the tube with glue and roll the black paper around it. They should hold the paper on the tube for a few seconds, allowing the glue to set.

5. Have the students trim the tip end of the sword.

6. Help the children cut a hole in the plastic cottage cheese container lid just large enough for the tube to slip through.

7. Show how to trace the lid on colored paper and cut out two circles, then glue one to each side of the lid.

8. Have the students write the memory verse on the top side of the inner lid.

9. Demonstrate how to slide the ring over the bottom of the tube, leaving approximately 4" extended for the handle. They can secure the lid with glue if necessary.

Changing Water to Wine

Ages 8-11

Memory Verse

Jesus said to the servants, fill the jars with water.

~John 2:7

....

First Miracle

Jesus was at a wedding with His mother and the disciples. The wine that they were serving ran out. They came to Jesus and asked what to do. Nearby were six stone water jars, so Jesus instructed the servants to fill them to the brim with water. When they had done this, He told them to take some from the top and serve it to the master of the banquet.

When the master tasted it, he was amazed because it was no longer water but wine. And it was better than any wine he had tasted before! So he asked the bridegroom, "Why did you save the best wine until now? Usually you serve the best first and save the cheaper wine for last."

This was the very first miracle that Jesus performed. It revealed that He truly had God's power and blessings. The disciples put their faith in Him.

— based on John 2:1-11

For Discussion

1. Where was Jesus when they ran out of wine?

2. What happened to the water in the jars?

3. What did this miracle reveal about Jesus?

Create • Take • Create • Take • Create • Take • Create • Take • Create

Egg Shell Crack Pots

What You Need

- egg shells
- water
- food coloring
- vinegar
- newspaper
- paper towels
- craft glue
- small plastic juice bottles
- resealable plastic sandwich bags
- craft sticks
- waxed paper

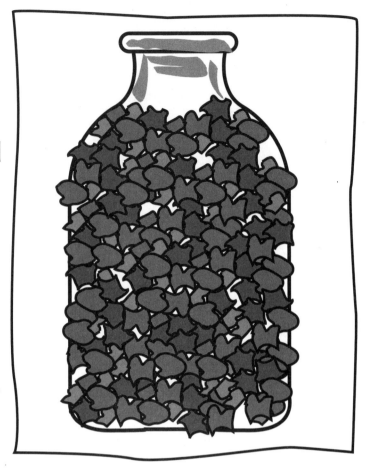

Before Class

Boil several eggs and peel the shells from them. Wash and dry the shells thoroughly. Mix together two cups of boiling water, three or four drops of food coloring and one tablespoon of vinegar. Put all of the ingredients in a glass bowl and soak the egg shells in it for a half-hour. Take the shells out and allow them to dry on newspaper topped with paper towels. Place several egg shells in a sandwich bag for each child.

What to Do

1. Give each child a sandwich bag with egg shells in it. Have them close the top and crunch up the shells.

2. Give the students a small plastic juice bottle. Working over waxed paper, have them spread a layer of glue on one side of the bottle using a craft stick.

3. Show how to sprinkle the egg shells all over the side. Instruct the students to not touch the glue with their fingers or the shells will stick to them rather than the jars. They should turn the jar and repeat until all four sides are covered.

4. Allow drying time before sending the project home.

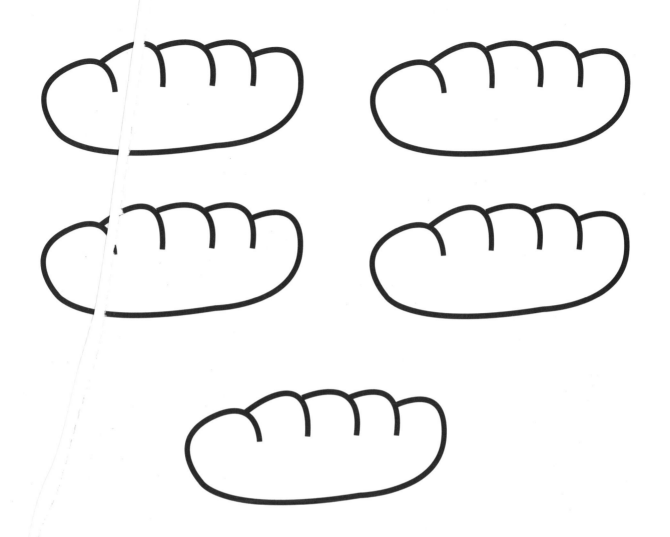

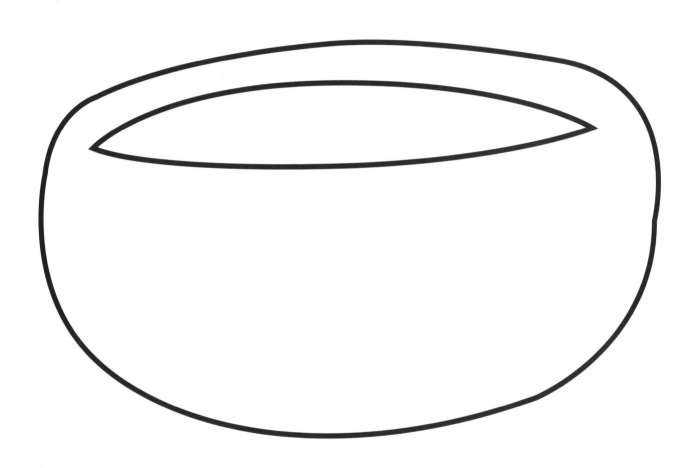

The Good Samaritan

Ages 8-11

Memory Verse

Love your neighbor as yourself.

~Matthew 19:19

· ·

Kindness

Jesus was asked, "Who is my neighbor?" So He told this parable. A man was on his way to Jericho when he was attacked by robbers who beat him, took his clothes and possessions and left him in a ditch to die.

A priest came by a short time later. When he saw the man, he hurried across the road and kept walking. Then a Levite came along and also pretended not to see the man.

But then a Samaritan happened to come that way. He was a kind man. When he saw the wounded man, he stopped. He bandaged his wounds, put him on his own donkey and took him to an inn. He even paid the innkeeper to look after the man.

After the story, Jesus asked, "Who do you think was the real neighbor to this man?" Of course they said the Samaritan, who had mercy on him. Jesus told them to go out and do the same.

That is a commandment for us today. Treat your neighbor like you want to be treated. Your neighbor is anyone around you who has a need. It is our responsibility to help our neighbors and to show kindness to anyone, just as Christ would.

— based on Luke 10:25-37

For Discussion

1. What happened to the man on his way to Jericho?

2. Who stopped to help him?

3. Who are our neighbors?

A Lovely Wind Sock

What You Need

- pattern from page 21
- colored poster board
- crepe paper streamers
- yarn
- markers
- glue
- scissors
- hole punch
- ornament hooks

Before Class

Duplicate the pattern sheet for each child.

What to Do

1. Let the students color the pattern sheet with markers.

2. Have the students cut out the pattern sheet using the guide line and glue it to the center of a 9" x 15" piece of colored poster board.

3. Show how to roll the poster board into a cylinder and staple or glue the back seam.

4. Allow the children to cut six brightly-colored streamers from crepe paper and glue them to the inside bottom edge of the cylinder.

5. Instruct the students to punch four evenly-spaced holes in the top rim of the cylinder.

6. Have the students cut two 15" pieces of yarn and thread the yarn from one hole to the one directly across from it and tie a knot. They should repeat this method using the other two holes.

7. Show how to use an ornament hook to catch the two strings of yarn in the middle of the cylinder to make a hanger. Pull the knots inside first so they don't show.

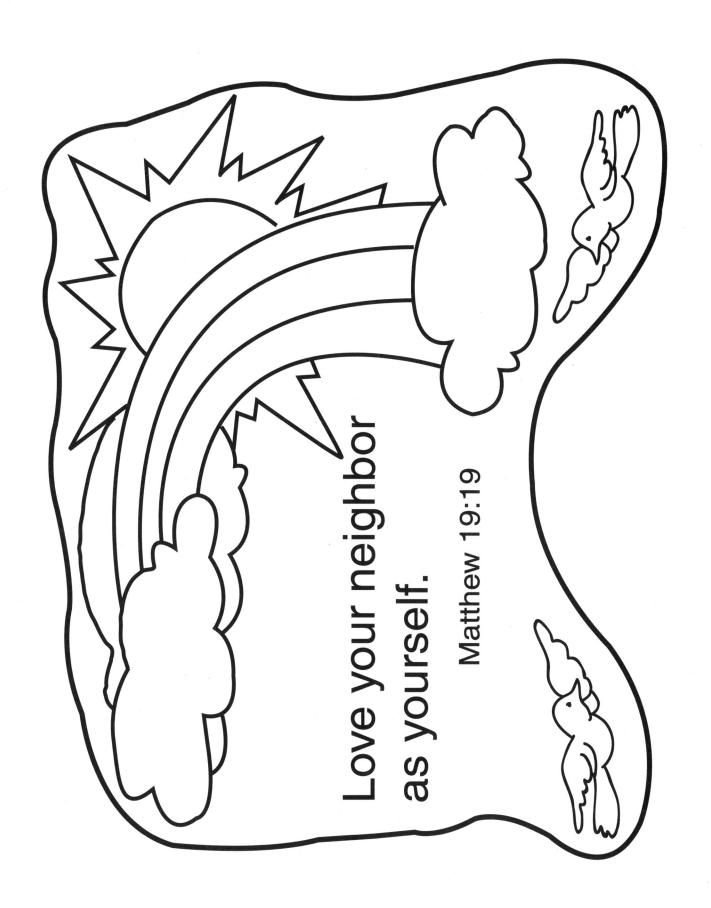

Love your neighbor as yourself.

Matthew 19:19

Healing a Blind Man

Ages 5-8

Memory Verse

Go…your faith has healed you.

~Mark 10:52

Faith

Many people heard of the miracles that Jesus performed when He walked on earth. One day as Jesus neared Jericho, a blind man named Bartimaeus sat by the road begging for money. When he heard it was Jesus passing by, he began to shout, "Jesus, Son of David, have mercy on me!" People told him to be quiet, but Jesus asked him what he wanted. Bartimaeus said, "I want to see!" Jesus told him that his faith had healed him. Immediately, he could see.

The Bible says that after Bartimaeus' sight was restored, he followed Jesus down the road. Bartimaeus had faith in Jesus. He knew that Jesus had the ability to heal him. All he needed to do was ask.

Jesus can still heal us today. He can meet all of our needs. All we have to do is ask Him and then believe He can do it. No need is too great for Him.

— based on Mark 10:46-52

For Discussion

1. Why was the man sitting by the road?

2. When the man found out Jesus was passing by, what did he do?

3. What do we need today for healing?

Create • Take • Create • Take • Create • Take • Create • Take • Create

Perfect Pin Hole Picture

What You Need

- church pattern from page 24
- black construction paper
- folded towels or carpet scraps
- blunt yarn needles
- small transparency sheets
- scissors
- paper clips
- permanent markers

Before Class

Go... your faith has healed you!

Mark 10:52

Duplicate the church pattern for each child. Cut a 3½" x 3" piece of transparency sheet for each child.

What to Do

1. Give each student a church and have them cut out the circle, then paper clip the pattern to the black construction paper.

2. Instruct the children to lay the sheets on a soft surface such as a scrap of carpet or some folded towels. Using a blunt yarn needle, show how to poke holes through the pattern into the black paper, outlining the church. (Make sure the needle pokes all the way through.)

3. Have the students remove the white pattern sheet. They should cut out the black circle above the church doors.

4. Give each child a pre-cut transparency sheet. Show how to tape it to the back of the church, covering the cut out opening. Allow the students to use a permanent marker to write the memory verse on the "window."

5. Encourage the students to take the picture home and hang it in a window so the light can shine through the holes.

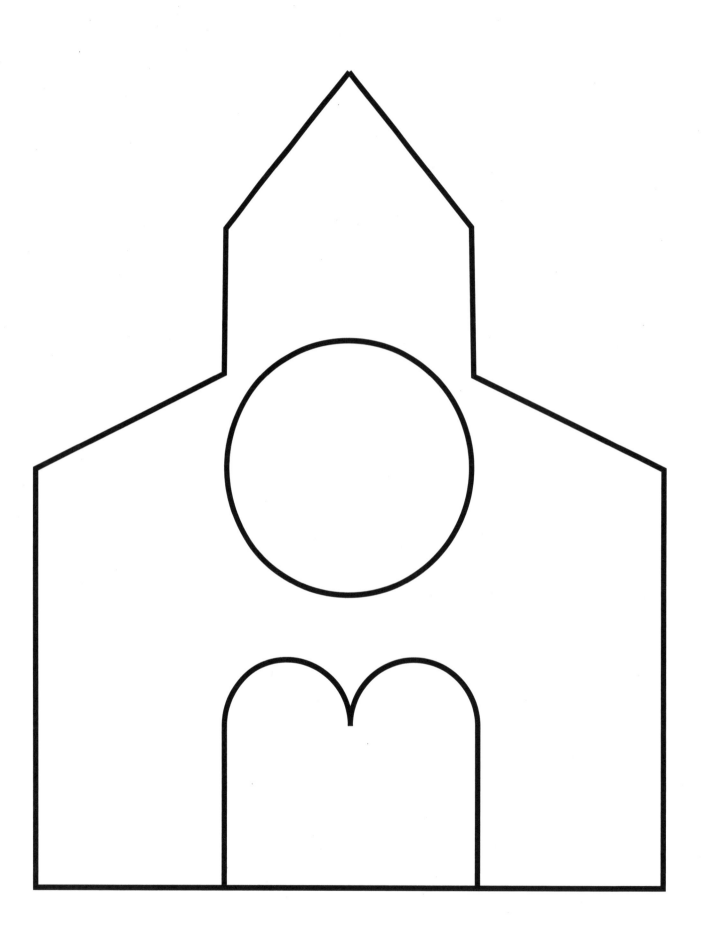

Healing a Paralytic

Ages 5-8

Memory Verse

I tell you, get up, take up your mat and go home.

~Mark 2:11

• •

Belief

Wherever Jesus went, crowds of people came to hear Him preach and teach. Many came for healing. One day when He was in Capernaum He spoke inside a house. It was so full that no one else could get in.

Four men came to the house carrying a paralytic man. "Paralytic" means he could not walk, so his friends carried him on a stretcher. They believed that if they could just get through the crowd to Jesus that the man could be healed. But there were too many people, so they had to come up with a new plan. They took the man up on the roof and dug down through it, making a large opening. Then they lowered the man down, right in front of Jesus.

When Jesus saw their faith, He said, "Son, your sins are forgiven." Then He told the paralytic to take his mat and go home. The man joyously obeyed Him.

Jesus was impressed by the faith these men had. They believed He could heal their friend. They did not give up until they found a way to get him to Jesus. Would you do the same for your friends?

— based on Mark 2:1-12

For Discussion

1. What does "paralytic" mean?

2. How did the friends get the man to Jesus?

3. What did their actions show?

Create • Take • Create • Take • Create • Take • Create • Take • Create

Courage on a Cot

What You Need

- chenille stems
- chenille bumps
- plastic drinking straws
- felt
- yarn
- self-stick labels

Before Class

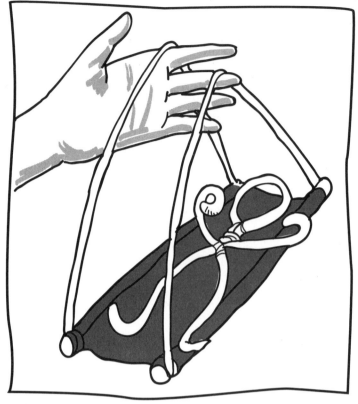

Practice constructing a man using a chenille stem and a chenille bump. Consult the diagram below. Cut yarn into 24" lengths, one per child.

What to Do

1. Show how to construct the man using a chenille stem and a chenille bump.

2. Have the students cut a rectangle from felt that is approximately 6"x 4".

3. Instruct the children to apply glue liberally to one edge of the felt lengthwise and roll one straw up in it. Repeat on the other side, leaving a 2" opening in the center for the man to lie on.

4. Show how to thread a 24" piece of yarn through the straw and tie the ends together. Repeat for the other side.

5. Have the students write the memory verse on a self-stick label and put it on the under side of the mat.

6. They should place the man on the mat.

Step 1 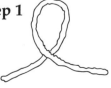   **Step 2**   **Step 3** 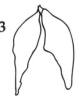   **Step 4**

Healing an Epileptic Boy

Ages 8-11

Memory Verse

Everything is possible for him who believes.

~Mark 9:23

Belief

A boy who had epilepsy was brought to Jesus. Epilepsy is a disease that causes seizures. When epileptics have seizures, they become stiff, toss themselves about and sometimes foam at the mouth. Today, doctors have medicine to help control epilepsy, but in Bible times people with this disease were thought to have an evil spirit living in them. That is what the people thought about this boy. The disciples had tried to drive out the "evil spirit," but they couldn't.

The boy had a seizure in front of Jesus. Jesus asked how long the boy had suffered from seizures and his father said, "Since he was a child. So if there is anything You can do, help him!" Jesus reminded the man that he only had to put his trust in Him. He said to the man, "Everything is possible to those who believe." Quickly, the father declared, "I do believe!" and Jesus healed his son.

Sometimes it is hard to believe in things we can't see, but Jesus is all-powerful. He can do anything. Faith is believing what God says He will do. If it is written in His word, we know it is true.

— based on Mark 9:14-32

For Discussion

1. What was wrong with the boy brought to Jesus?

2. Who had tried to help him?

3. Why did Jesus heal the boy?

4. Why is faith so important?

Believer's Plaque

What You Need

- plastic or foam meat trays
- craft glue
- gold or silver foil
- soda can tabs
- sequins
- markers

Before Class

No preparation needed.

What to Do

1. Help the students cut an inside liner for the plastic or foam tray from gold or silver foil paper and glue it to the tray.

2. Instruct the children to write the memory verse on the back of the tray, with a marker.

3. Show how to use craft glue to write BELIEVE in large letters inside the tray one letter at a time.

4. Have the students glue colored sequins to the letters and add a few others around to decorate the plaque. The star-shaped ones work well.

5. After allowing a short drying time, show how to glue or tape the soda can tab to the center top back for a hanger.

Create & Take
Bible Crafts

Jesus and the Children

Ages 5-8

Memory Verse

Let the little children come to me.

~Mark 10:14

Compassion

When Jesus was ministering on earth, crowds of people followed Him wherever He went. Some came for healing, some to see the miracles and some just to hear His teaching.

One day, little children were brought to Jesus by their parents so He could bless them. Can you imagine how excited those kids must have been to be close to Jesus? But the disciples tried to push them away and told them to sit down. As soon as Jesus saw what the disciples were doing, He stopped them.

"Let the children come to Me and don't hinder them," He told them. "They belong to the kingdom of God." Then He took the children in His arms and blessed them.

Did you know that Jesus still cares about children today? You can go to Him in prayer and He will take care of your needs. No one is too small or unimportant to Jesus. He loves all the children everywhere. He blesses them when they go to Him.

— based on Mark 10:13-16

For Discussion

1. Why did the disciples try to push the children away?

2. What was Jesus' response?

3. How can children talk to Jesus today?

Create • Take • Create • Take • Create • Take • Create • Take • Create

All the Children of the World Mobile

What You Need

- patterns from page 31
- crayons
- scissors
- glue
- small foil pans
- string or heavy thread
- ornament hooks
- hole punch

Before Class

Duplicate the pattern page, two per child. Cut five 12" lengths and one 24" length of thread per child.

What to Do

1. Have the children color both pattern sheets and cut out the children and world.

2. Have the students lay one set of pictures face down, spread them with glue and lay one 12" string down the middle. Show how to place the matching picture face-up on top of the glue. (Be sure the faces are not upside-down and the string is coming out of the top center.)

3. Instruct the children to assemble the world using the same method and the 24" length of string.

4. Show to turn a small foil pan upside-down and poke two small holes in the top center for the ornament hook. Help the students insert the hook in the holes and twist the ends together. Assist in tying the thread for the globe to the underneath side of the hook.

5. Help the children use a hole punch to make five holes around the rim of the aluminum pan. They should tie one thread with the children to each hole.

6. Write or have the students write the memory verse on both sides of the globe.

Jesus Appears to Thomas

Ages 8-11

Memory Verse

Blessed are those who have not seen and yet have believed.

~John 20:29

Belief Without Seeing

After Jesus rose from the dead, He appeared to the disciples. They saw Him and believed that He was alive. One of the disciples, Thomas, had not been with them though, so when they told him about seeing Jesus, Thomas did not believe them. He said that unless he saw the nail prints in Jesus' hands and the hole in Jesus' side, he could not believe his Lord was alive.

About a week later the disciples were together in a house with all of the doors locked. Suddenly, Jesus appeared in the middle of them. He told Thomas to touch His hands and His side so he could stop doubting. When Thomas saw Him, he believed.

Then Jesus told the disciples, "Because you see, you believe. But blessed are those who have not seen Me, yet they believe."

We cannot physically see Jesus today as the disciples did, but we can believe because the Bible tells us He is alive. We can feel His presence and see the miracles He is still doing today. We can believe without seeing. Jesus says we are blessed for doing so.

— based on John 20:24-31

For Discussion

1. Why didn't Thomas believe the other disciples?

2. What made Thomas believe Jesus was alive?

3. How do we know Jesus is alive today?

Picture Perfect Frame

What You Need

- frame and stand from page 34
- heavy poster board
- thin poster board
- scissors
- glue
- markers
- star stickers

Before Class

Duplicate the frame and stand for each child.

What to Do

1. Have the students use the pattern to trace and cut the outer edges of the frame from heavy poster board.

2. They should repeat the process on thin poster board, although this time they should trace the center of the frame and cut it out.

3. Show how to glue the top and side edges of the frame to the heavy poster board. (Do not glue across the bottom.)

4. Allow the students to outline the edges of the frame with a marker and add star stickers to decorate it.

5. Have the students write the memory verse across the top back of the frame.

6. Have the students use the pattern to trace and cut the stand from heavy poster board. Show how to fold and glue it to the lower middle of the back of the frame. Allow it to dry before standing the frame upright.

7. Encourage the children to slip their favorite photo into the slot on the bottom of the frame.

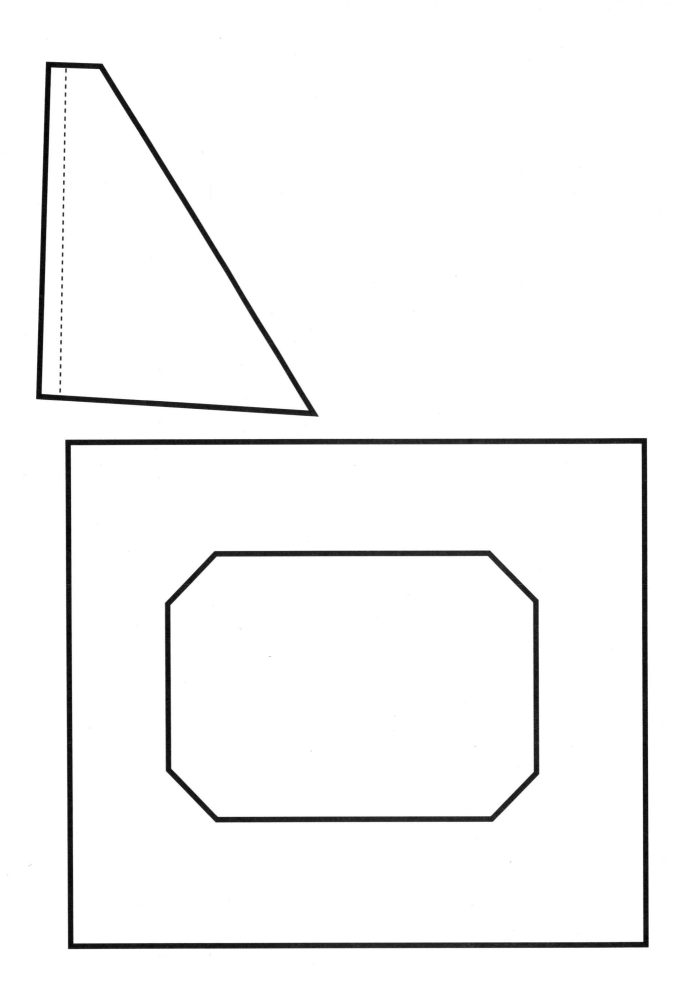

Jesus Calms the Sea

Ages 5-8

Memory Verse

You of little faith, why are you so afraid?

~Matthew 8:26

....

Doubt

Sometimes after Jesus taught, He became tired and needed a little time away from the people. One such day, He and the disciples went out on the lake in a boat.

A furious storm began to rock the boat. The disciples were afraid it would tip over. They hurried to wake up Jesus, who was asleep. He scolded them for their doubt and for not having faith. Then He told the wind and storm to stop. Everything became calm.

The disciples were amazed, but Jesus was disappointed that the men had doubted Him. He is disappointed with us, too, when we doubt that He has the ability to calm the storms in our lives.

— based on Matthew 8:23-27

For Discussion

1. Why was Jesus in the boat?

2. What happened while He was sleeping?

3. What was Jesus' reaction when the disciples woke Him?

Create • Take • Create • Take • Create • Take • Create • Take • Create

Anchors Away

What You Need

- anchor pattern from page 37
- gray or brown construction paper
- scissors
- glue
- markers

Before Class

Duplicate the anchor pattern for each child.

Within the illustration:

You of little faith, why are you so afraid?

Matthew 8:26

What to Do

1. Give each child a sheet of construction paper to fold lengthwise.

2. Have the students trace the anchor on the folded paper and cut it out, being careful not to cut the fold.

3. Instruct the children to write the memory verse down the center of the anchor with a marker.

4. Help the students cut construction paper strips about ½" x 4" in size and glue them into loops for a chain. They should attach the chain through the hole in the top of the anchor.

Create & Take Bible Crafts

Jesus Is Alive!

Ages 5-8

Memory Verse

He is not here; he has risen!

~Matthew 28:6

Death to Life

It was a very sad day when Jesus was crucified on the cross. The Bible says the sky turned dark that day. The earth was still and silent. No birds sang. But that wasn't the end of the story — it was just the beginning!

When Jesus' body was placed in the tomb, a huge stone was rolled in front of the opening. Yet that was not the end either. In just three days, that big stone was rolled away and the tomb was found to be empty. Jesus was alive again!

You can read in the Bible about all of the miracles that Jesus performed while He was here on earth. They were marvelous miracles that showed His power. But the greatest miracle of all was when Jesus died for our sins and rose again. Death could not defeat our Lord. He began a new life with His Father in heaven.

Sin does not have to defeat us either. If we ask forgiveness, we can begin new lives as children of God. Then some day we, too, will be living in heaven with Him.

— based on Matthew 28:1-10

For Discussion

1. What happened to the earth the day Jesus was crucified?

2. How long was Jesus in the tomb?

3. Why can't sin defeat us?

Create • Take • Create • Take • Create • Take • Create • Take • Create

Notable Sewing Card

What You Need

- patterns from page 40
- colored poster board
- glue
- markers
- clear, self-stick plastic
- scissors
- hole punch
- yarn

Before Class

Duplicate the patterns for each child. Cut a 48" length of yarn for each child and tape the ends.

What to Do

1. Have the students cut out the music note, trace it on colored poster board and cut out that music note.

2. Have the children color the leaves and stamen on the lily. They should cut around the outside of the lily to cut it out, but not necessarily flush. Show where to glue the lily to the rounded part of the music note.

3. Instruct the children to write the memory verse on the top and middle of the note.

4. Help the students cover the note with clear, self-stick plastic and trim the edges.

5. Show how to punch holes around the outside of the note with a hole punch.

6. Give each child a pre-cut length of yarn to "sew" around the music note.

Create · Take · Create · Take · Create · Take · Create · Take · Create

The Lamp

Ages 5-8

Memory Verse

Your eye is the lamp of your body.

~Luke 11:34

....

Light

In another parable, Jesus told about a lamp. He said that it would be silly to light a lamp and then hide it under something. Instead, we should place it on a table or stand so that everyone who comes in can see it.

Then He said that our eyes are the lamps of our bodies. When our eyes look at good things, our whole bodies will be full of light. But if our eyes look at bad or evil things, then our bodies will be full of darkness.

We must be careful, then, that we only put light within us and not darkness. If we hide away little sins, the corners of our lives will not be lighted. Just as the lamp on the table needs to be uncovered to give off its full light, we need to be free of the darkness of sin to be a light to those around us.

— based on Luke 11:33-36

For Discussion

1. What does Jesus say are the "lamps of our bodies"? Why?

2. What happens when we look at good things?

3. Name some sins that cause darkness inside us.

Create • Take • Create • Take • Create • Take • Create • Take • Create

An Open Book

Your eye is the lamp of your body. Luke 11:34

What You Need

- Bible and lamp patterns from pages 43 and 44
- construction paper
- 7" red ribbons
- scissors
- glue
- markers

Before Class

Duplicate the pattern pages for each child.

What to Do

1. Have the students cut out the Bible pattern and trace it on black construction paper, then cut it out.

2. Instruct the children to then cut the center page section from the Bible pattern.

3. They should outline the white "pages" with a thick red marker.

4. Have the students color the lamp with markers, cut it out and glue it to the right side of the white pages.

5. They should write the memory verse on the left side of the open Bible.

6. Show how to fold the white page in half, run a line of glue down the under side of the crease and attach it to the black Bible cover.

7. Demonstrate how to drop a dab of glue to each outside corner of the white page and bend it slightly inward before attaching it to the black paper.

8. Allow the students to glue a 7" piece of red ribbon down the center of the Bible.

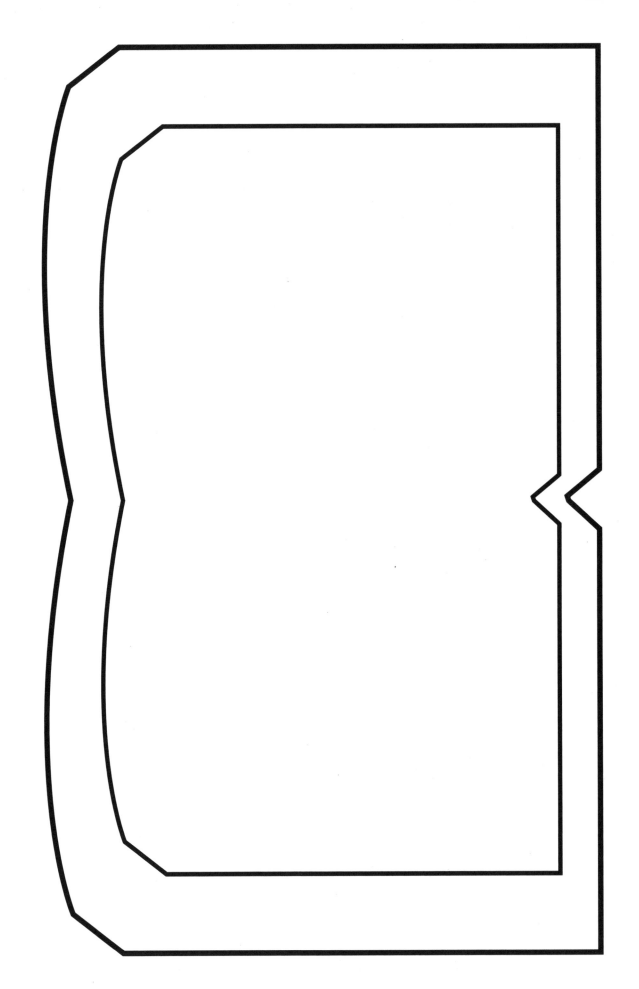

44

The Lilies and the Birds

Ages 8-11

Memory Verse

Who of you by worrying can add a single hour to his life?

~Luke 12:25

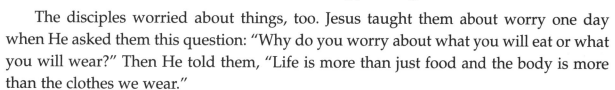

Worry

Do you ever worry about things? Things like: "What am I going to wear to school tomorrow?" or "What will I have for supper tonight?"

The disciples worried about things, too. Jesus taught them about worry one day when He asked them this question: "Why do you worry about what you will eat or what you will wear?" Then He told them, "Life is more than just food and the body is more than the clothes we wear."

Jesus compared the disciples to the lilies that grow in the fields and the birds that fly in the sky. They do not worry how they look, yet they are beautiful. The birds don't store up food in barns, but they have plenty to eat because their heavenly Father provides for them.

If God cares about the birds and the flowers, how much more He must care for our needs! Worrying will not make anything better. It only drags us down. We are more valuable to God than the birds and lilies. We do not need to worry because God will take care of us.

— based on Luke 12:22-34

For Discussion

1. Why shouldn't we worry about clothes or food?

2. How are the birds taken care of?

3. What happens when we worry?

Birds in a Tree

What You Need

- bird and tree patterns from page 47
- green, blue and black construction paper
- scissors
- glue
- markers
- hole punch

Before Class

Duplicate the patterns for each child.

Who of you by worrying can add a single hour to his life?
Luke 12:25

What to Do

1. Have the children cut out the patterns.

2. Instruct each child to trace and cut one tree from a piece of folded green construction paper and trace and cut two birds from blue construction paper.

3. Show how to turn one bird each way and glue on a small black eye made by using a hole punch on black paper. They should bend the wing down over the bird's side.

4. Have the students unfold the tree. Show how to cut two large slashes, one on each side of the tree, and place the birds in the tree.

5. Instruct the children to write the memory verse in the middle of the tree.

Create & Take Bible Crafts

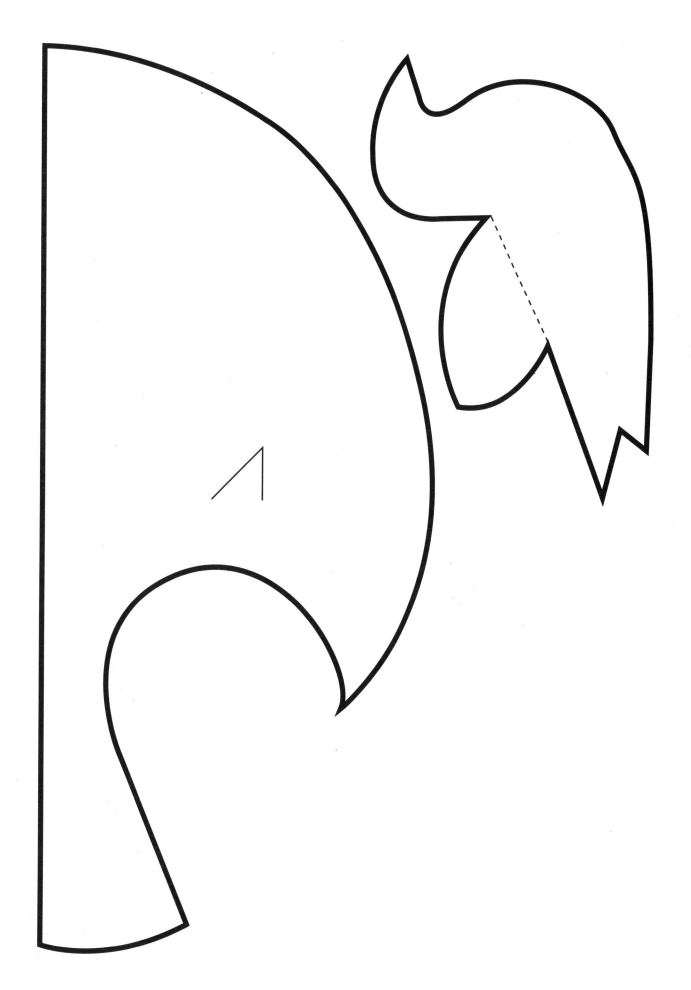

47

Lost Coin

Ages 5-8

Memory Verse

Seek and you will find.

~Matthew 7:7

Searching

A woman had 10 silver coins. She lost one. Do you think she said, "Oh, well, at least I have nine left?" No, she didn't! She lit a lamp, got out her broom and searched and cleaned her house until she found the one coin that was missing! Then she rejoiced.

There are millions of people in the world. Many of them are lost because they don't know Jesus. But did you know that He is searching for each one who is lost? Even though there are lots of Christians already, God still cares about those who are not following Him. He never gives up looking for them.

The Bible says that the angels rejoice over one sinner who repents and is brought to God, just as the woman rejoiced over finding her one lost coin. We can help others find Him, too.

— based on Luke 15:8-10

For Discussion

1. How much money did the woman lose?

2. How did she find it?

3. Why does God search for one lost person?

Create • Take • Create • Take • Create • Take • Create • Take • Create

Marvelous Magnifying Glass

What You Need

- magnifying glass pattern from page 50
- thin, colored poster board
- scissors
- glue
- markers
- plastic transparency sheets

Before Class

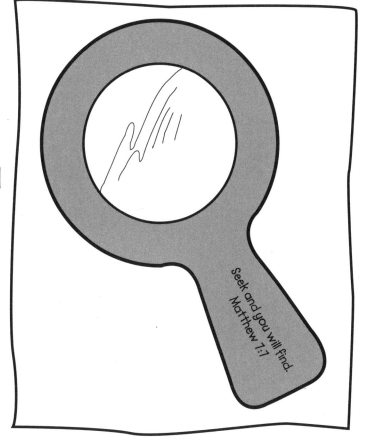

Seek and you will find. Matthew 7:7

Use the magnifying glass pattern from page 50 to cut a template from cardboard. Cut the transparencies into 4½" x 4½" square, one per child.

What to Do

1. Have each child use the template to trace and cut two magnifying glasses from colored poster board. Show how to cut out and remove the center circles.

2. Show how to apply glue to the outer ring of one magnifying glass and set the plastic over the hole.

3. Have the students apply glue to the outer edges of the other ring and set it down on the first one. If the plastic edges show, help the students trim them off.

4. Instruct the children to write the memory verse on the handle. If they choose dark poster board they can write with a white crayon.

Create · Take · Create · Take · Create · Take · Create · Take · Create

The Lost Sheep

Ages 5-8

Memory Verse

He cares for you.

~1 Peter 5:7

....

Caring Shepherd

Do you like stories? Jesus often told stories to people. Stories helped them understand the lessons He tried to teach.

In one story, He told about a man who had 100 sheep. One night when the man counted the sheep, one was missing. Even though he still had 99 sheep, the man searched until he found the one that was lost.

We are like God's sheep. He cares for us. If we stray away from Him, He wants us back even though He has lots of other people to love. We are that important to Him! He cares for us.

— based on Luke 15:1-17

For Discussion

1. Why did the man in the story look for one lost sheep?

2. How are we like sheep?

3. How important are we to God?

Create • Take • Create • Take • Create • Take • Create • Take • Create

Sponge-Painted Sheep

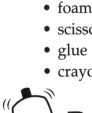

What You Need

- patterns from page 53
- 12" x 18" sheets of blue construction paper
- green and white tempera paint
- paint smocks
- sponges
- spring-type clothespins
- foam meat trays
- scissors
- glue
- crayons

He cares for you. 1 Peter 5:7

Before Class

Duplicate the patterns from page 53 for each child. Cut the sponges into approximately 1½" circles. You will need two foam meat trays.

What to Do

1. Have the children cut out the two patterns.

2. Give each child a 12" x 18" sheet of blue construction paper. Instruct them to trace the sheep pattern in the center of the paper.

3. The students should trace a tree trunk on each side of the sheep and color the trunks brown. Instruct them to leave room at the top of the trunk for foliage.

4. Have the students put on smocks to protect their clothing. Show how to pinch the clothespins onto the backs of the sponge circles to hold them for painting. Place a small amount of green paint on one meat tray and white on the other.

5. Instruct the children to dab the sponge up and down in the tray of white paint and touch it to the paper to make fluffy sheep. Do not stroke as you would with a paint brush. They should continue until the sheep are covered, then repeat the same method using green for the tree tops.

6. After the paint has dried, instruct the students to add black eyes and pink ears to the sheep. They should write the memory verse across the bottom of the page.

The Mustard Seed

Ages 5-8

Memory Verse

The apostles said to the Lord, "Increase our faith!"

~Luke 17:5

●●●●●●●●●●●●●●●●●●●●●●●●●●●●●●

Faith

Have you ever seen a mustard seed? It is a very, very tiny seed. It is round and sort of a greenish-brown color. But even with its small size it can be very powerful. It has a pungent flavor used for seasoning foods.

The Bible says that when the mustard seed is planted, it becomes one of the biggest plants in the whole garden. A mustard seed becomes a tree large enough for birds to build their nests.

When Jesus spoke of faith in Luke 17:16 and in Matthew 17:20, He told the disciples that if they would have faith as big as a mustard seed, they could move mountains. Faith is believing. Even a small amount of faith can accomplish great things when used for God. Even greater faith means even more wonderful things can happen with God's help. What size is your faith?

— based on Luke 13:18-21

For Discussion

1. Describe a mustard seed.

2. For what is the mustard seed used?

3. How is faith like a mustard seed?

Create • Take • Create • Take • Create • Take • Create • Take • Create

Mustard Seed Puppet Pics

What You Need

- patterns from page 56
- construction paper
- 3½" craft sticks
- tape
- scissors
- green, tan or brown pom-poms
- wiggle eyes
- craft glue
- stapler

A mustard seed is oh, so small,
I can hardly see it at all!
But when it's planted in the ground,
A mighty tree will soon abound.
If our faith is as big as that seed,
God will meet our every need.

Before Class

Duplicate the verse on colored paper for each child. Make cardboard templates of the tree top and trunk using the patterns. Each child will need one sheet of 9" x 7" construction paper, two wiggle eyes and two 3½" craft sticks.

What to Do

1. Have the students glue two wiggle eyes to a small green, brown or tan pom-pom, then glue the pom-pom to a 3½" craft stick.

2. Instruct the students to use the tree templates to trace and cut them from the appropriate colors of construction paper and glue them together. Show how to tape a 3½-inch craft stick to the very bottom of the tree trunk.

3. Show how to cut a 2½" by 2½" corner from the 9" x 7" sheet of construction paper (where the seed will peek through), then fold up and staple the sides. Show how to cut two notches out of the bottom of the fold (for the sticks) as shown.

4. Allow the children to use a brown crayon or marker to color "soil" on the lower left side of the paper. Show how to slide the craft stick with the mustard seed on it through the notch.

5. Have the students slide the tree into the other notch. (The tree should remain hidden until the poem is read.)

6. Instruct the children to glue the poem to the right side of the pocket, then write the memory verse on the back. Practice telling the story with the children so that they will be able to re-tell it to their parents.

A mustard seed is oh, so small,

I can hardly see it at all!

But when it's planted in the ground,

A mighty tree will soon abound.

If our faith is as big as that seed,

God will meet our every need.

The Net

Ages 8-11

Memory Verse

Evil men will bow down in the presence of the good.

~Proverbs 14:19

. . . .

Separating Good from Bad

Because the disciples were familiar with fishing, Jesus used fishing stories to teach them lessons. In one of His parables He talked about a net. The disciples all knew that a net was used to catch fish. The fisherman dropped a huge net into the water alongside his boat, then pulled it up, trapping all kinds of different fish in it. Afterward, he separated the good fish from the bad fish. A fisherman could sell the good ones, but the bad ones had to be thrown away.

It was easy for Jesus to use the net as a comparison for the kingdom of heaven. He told the disciples that the time will come when all people must be "sorted," too. The good ones will enter heaven, but the bad ones will be thrown into fire. Living for Jesus is the only way to assure that you will be found to be a "good fish" when the final net is pulled in.

— based on Matthew 13:47-52

For Discussion

1. How do you use a net to catch fish?

2. What is the first thing you do once fish are caught?

3. What happened to "bad" fish?

4. How do we compare to fish?

Create · Take · Create · Take · Create · Take · Create · Take · Create

Net Full O' Fish

What You Need

- fish patterns from pages 59 and 60
- 10" x 12" sheets of poster board
- crayons or markers
- netting
- scissors
- glue
- packaging tape

Before Class

Duplicate the fish patterns for each child. Onion or apple bags work well for the netting. You can also purchase netting in fabric and craft stores.

What to Do

1. Let the students color the fish patterns with crayons or markers. Encourage them to make the fish as colorful as possible so they will stand out behind the netting.

2. Instruct the students to cut out the fish and glue them to a sheet of poster board.

3. Show how to cut off the ends of an onion or apple sack and stretch it as long and wide as possible so that it lays flat.

4. Instruct the children to cover the fish picture with the netting. Allow them to use extra wide tape to secure the net all the way around the poster board. They should make sure that all the ragged edges of the net are taped.

5. Have the students write the memory verse on the back of the paper.

Create • Take • Create • Take • Create • Take • Create • Take • Create

Pearl of Great Price

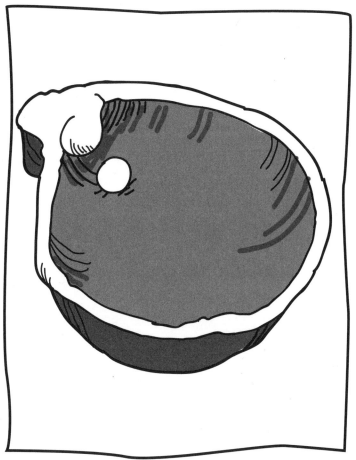

Ages 8-11

Memory Verse

He found one pearl of great price.

~Matthew 13:46 KJV

....

Our Value

Pearls are hard, lustrous gems that are formed inside oyster shells. In ancient times, they were among the most precious gems and were highly esteemed as ornaments. They are still worth a lot of money and are considered very valuable. Perhaps your mom owns a pearl necklace or earrings.

In one of Jesus' parables, He told of a man who found a pearl while he was walking in a field. The man wanted that pearl so much that he sold all he had so that he could buy the field and therefore own the pearl.

Jesus tells us the kingdom of heaven is like that. It is of such great value that we should be willing to give up all we have to make our home in heaven. We will not "own" heaven, but we can know that we will have a place there when we die. We can be with Jesus, who is worth more than all the pearls in the world.

— Matthew 13:44-46

For Discussion

1. Where are pearls found?

2. To what does Jesus compare a pearl?

3. Who is worth more than pearls?

Create • Take • Create • Take • Create • Take • Create • Take • Create

Priceless Pearl Magnet

What You Need

- patterns from page 63
- craft foam
- thin poster board
- craft glue
- scissors
- mini pom-poms
- costume pearls
- magnets
- markers

He found one pearl of great price.
Matthew 13:46

Before Class

Duplicate the patterns for each child. You will need five pom-poms per student. If craft foam is not available, you can use colored meat trays or construction paper for this craft. You can purchase a string of beads at a craft store or garage sale that make suitable "pearls."

What to Do

1. Have the students use the patterns to trace and cut one flower (any color) and two leaves (green) from craft foam.

2. They should outline the flower shape with a coordinating color of marker.

3. Show how to glue the five mini pom-poms in a circle on the center of the flower. Give each student one pearl to glue in the center of the circle.

4. Have the students cut a background shape from poster board using the guide provided. They should outline the edges with a color that will compliment their flower.

5. Show how to lay the flower and leaves on the cut-out (but do not yet glue them) and write the memory verse on it.

6. Allow the students to glue the flower and leaves on the front and a magnet on the back.

The Persistent Widow

Ages 5-8

Memory Verse

Pray continually!

~1 Thessalonians 5:17

Don't Give Up

In the book of Luke there is a story Jesus told about a judge. This judge did not care about people and he did not honor God. A widow came to him and asked for justice. At first he ignored her pleas, but she would not give up! She kept returning with her request until the judge finally gave in and granted her desire.

Jesus told the disciples that they must be like the widow. He said they should pray to God when they had a need. He said they should not give up until they received an answer from God.

God will bring justice to His children if we are faithful and continue to pray to Him. We must remember that God will answer our prayers the way He sees fit. This does not mean we will get all we want, but we will have our needs met. Remember to pray continually.

— based on Luke 18:1-8

For Discussion

1. What does "persistent" mean?

2. How can we be persistent?

3. Does persistence mean God will give us everything we want?

Create • Take • Create • Take • Create • Take • Create • Take • Create

Shoe Strings 'N' Straws Necklace

What You Need

- medallion pattern from page 66
- plastic drinking straws
- white poster board
- red or white shoe strings
- wooden beads
- scissors
- hole punch
- marker

Before Class

Duplicate the medallion pattern for each child.

What to Do

1. Have the students cut plastic drinking straws into six pieces each, approximately 1½" long.

2. Show how to use the pattern to trace and cut out the medallion from thin white poster board. The students should use a red marker to outline the edges and write the memory verse in the middle of the medallion.

3. Have the children punch two holes in the medallion as indicated on the pattern. Show how to thread the shoe string through the holes, leaving the medallion to hang in the center.

4. Demonstrate how to thread one bead on the string on each side of the medallion, followed by three straw pieces, another bead, three more straw pieces and ending with a bead.

5. Help the children tie the string ends together in a knot.

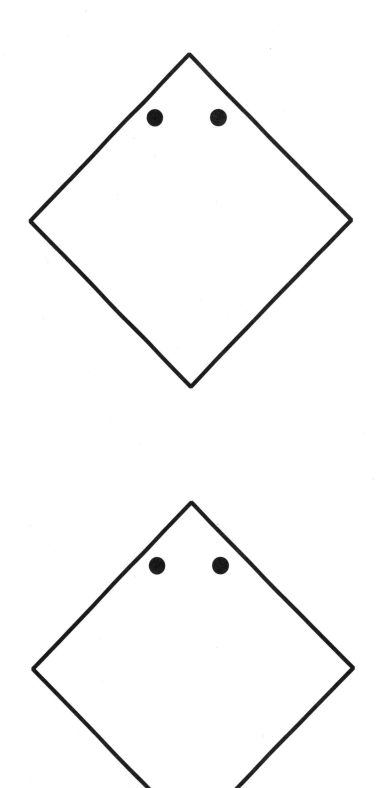

The Pharisee and the Tax Collector

Ages 8-11

Memory Verse

He who humbles himself will be exalted.

~Luke 18:14

....

Humility

Do you know what humility means? It means to not brag about yourself or be conceited. Jesus used a story about humility to teach some people who thought they were better than others.

According to the story, two men came to the temple to pray. One man stood up and proudly prayed about how good he was. He said he didn't steal or cheat or lie. He wanted everyone in the temple to hear his prayer.

But the other man quietly bowed his head and prayed to God, telling Him what a sinner he was.

God was not pleased with the first man's prayer, but He forgave the second man and exalted him. "Exalt" means "to lift up."

We must remember that God is greater than any of us. We are only what He has made us to be. It is wrong to think we are better than other people. God wants us to be humble.

— based on Luke 18:9-14

For Discussion

1. What is humility?

2. What does "exalted" mean?

3. Why should we be humble?

Create • Take • Create • Take • Create • Take • Create • Take • Create

Handy Note Pad

What You Need

- praying hands pattern from page 69
- thin poster board
- scissors
- stapler
- glue
- 3" x 3" squares of paper
- crayons
- clear, self-stick plastic
- magnets
- markers

Before Class

Duplicate a praying hands for each child. Make sure the magnets are large enough to hold the weight of the note pads.

What to Do

1. Have the children glue the praying hands sheet to thin poster board.

2. Allow the students to color the hands in a skin color.

3. Help the students cover the hands with clear, self-stick plastic and cut them out.

4. Give each child a small stack of 3" x 3" squares and let them staple the squares together with two staples at the top. Show how to smear a generous amount of glue on the back of the last sheet and glue the sheets to the center of the praying hands.

5. Encourage the students to write the memory verse on the back of the praying hands.

6. Give each child a magnet to glue to the back of the praying hands.

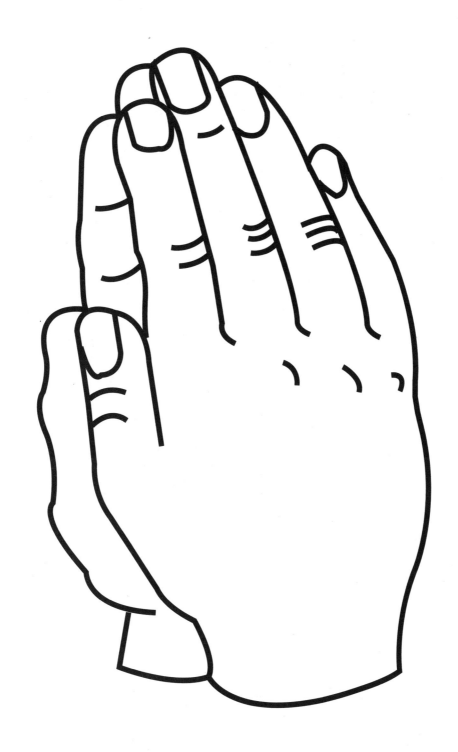

The Prodigal Son

Ages 8-11

Memory Verse

A friend loves at all times.

~Proverbs 17:17

. . . .

True Friends

What is a friend? Someone who likes you or is helpful to you? Sometimes we think people are friends, but later we find out they weren't true friends after all.

Another of Jesus' parables tells about a boy who decided he was old enough and smart enough to leave home, so he went to his dad and demanded his inheritance. Then he went to a big city and had all kinds of fun with his friends. They were glad to help him spend his money. But after the money ran out, so did the friends! The boy was penniless and all alone. He took a job feeding pigs. He became so hungry that he ate the pigs' food just to stay alive! He realized that even his father's servants ate better than that, so he decided to go home and beg his father for a job as a servant.

Sometimes the things of the world can look very inviting. There are always "friends" out there who are willing to hang around as long as everything is going well. But then when you are down, they are suddenly nowhere to be found. What kinds of friends do you have? Are they the kind of people Jesus would want you to be around? Do they do things that aren't right and then influence you to do wrong, too? Friends like that will only lead to trouble. Choose your friends carefully!

— based on Luke 15:11-31

For Discussion

1. Why did the son leave home?

2. What happened to him in the city?

3. Why is choosing good friends so important?

Piggy Napkin Holder

What You Need

- patterns for pig from page 72
- frozen juice cans
- pink tempera paint
- pink and other colors of construction paper
- white poster board
- markers
- scissors
- glue
- pink chenille wires
- wiggle eyes

A friend loves at all times.
Proverbs 17:17

Before Class

Duplicate the patterns for each child. Cut two 2" sections from the centers of the juice cans for the napkin to be inserted later. If the can is cardboard, paint it with pink tempera paint and allow it to dry. If the container is white plastic, leave it as it is.

What to Do

1. Have the students cut out the pig patterns.

2. Instruct the children to trace two pairs of legs on pink construction paper and two sets on poster board and cut them out. They should glue one pink set to each white set.

3. Instruct the children to cut one head, one snout, and two ears from pink construction paper. They may cut one hat from any color of paper they choose.

4. The students should glue one leg set to each end of the can.

5. Show how to assemble the face using two wiggle eyes and two hole punch dots for the nostrils.

6. Show how to cut a 2½" piece of chenille wire and curl it around a pencil for the tail. They should glue it to the back set of legs.

7. Have the students write the memory verse on the side of the pig with a marker.

Raising Lazarus

Ages 8-11

Memory Verse

Greater love has no one than this, that he lay down his life for his friends.

~John 15:13

. . . .

Love

Jesus had three friends named Mary, Martha and Lazarus. He visited their home many times. One day, He received word that Lazarus was very sick. Mary and Martha wanted Him to come right away and pray for their brother.

Jesus did not go immediately. He waited before making the journey to their home. When He got there, Lazarus was dead, but Jesus knew that already. He wanted to perform a miracle to build the people's faith.

Jesus asked to be taken to the tomb where Lazarus was buried. When He saw it, He wept. He told some men to roll away the stone that was used to seal the tomb. Martha protested that there would be a bad odor because Lazarus had been dead for a few days. Jesus responded that if they believed, they would see the glory of God.

The men removed the stone. Jesus called for His friend Lazarus to come forth. Lazarus came out of the tomb, still wrapped in his grave cloths. Jesus said, "Take off the grave cloths and let him go!"

Jesus loved His friend Lazarus very much. He loves each one of us very much, too. In fact, He loves us so much that He gave His life for us. That is why if we follow Him we can have eternal life in heaven.

— based on John 11:1-16

For Discussion

1. Who were Jesus friends?

2. Why didn't Jesus go to Lazarus right away?

3. What happened when Jesus called to His friends?

A Mummy's Cave

What You Need

- cave pattern from page 75
- brown paper bags
- white yarn
- thin craft sticks
- glue
- scissors
- markers
- 8½" x 6½" foam meat trays
- wooden clothespin (not spring-type)
- construction paper

Greater love has no one than this, that he lay down his life for his friend.

John 15:13

Before Class

Duplicate the cave pattern for each child.

What to Do

1. Have the students trace and cut one cave from a paper bag and one cave from construction paper using the pattern. They should glue them together with the paper bag side on top.

2. Allow the students to outline the cave with a black marker and write the memory verse on it.

3. Show how to cut a slot along the inside bottom rim of the tray, approximately 5" long and ¼" wide. Have the student set it aside.

4. Give each child a wooden clothespin. Show how to wrap white yarn around the clothespin from the top to the bottom, leaving just the "head" and "feet" exposed.

5. The students should wrap several layers of yarn around the clothespin and glue it in the back. Show how to glue a thin craft stick up inside the yarn, leaving about 1½"-2" extending down between the feet. Allow the students to draw two eyes on the "head" with a black marker.

6. Allow a couple of minutes for the clothespin to dry, then show how to slide Lazarus inside the foam tray with the craft stick inserted through the slot.

7. Show how to glue the cave to the outer rim of the tray, covering Lazarus.

8. Demonstrate how to slowly move Lazarus to appear in the doorway as the story is retold.

The Rich Fool

Ages 5-8

Memory Verse

A greedy man brings trouble to his family.

~Proverbs 15:27

Greed

Jesus told a parable about a prosperous farmer. One year the farmer's crops did very well and he didn't have enough room in his barns to store them all. But instead of sharing some of his "blessings" with others, he decided to build bigger barns so that he could keep everything himself! Then he planned to take life easy, just eating, drinking and partying.

But the story tells us that God had other plans for the greedy farmer. God said, "You fool, tonight you are going to die and then who will get all that you have stored up?"

Jesus used this story to warn us that if we choose to be selfish and greedy like the farmer, God will not be pleased with us, either. We need to be thankful for all the blessings that God gives us, but we also need to share those same blessings with others who may not have as much as we do. Don't be greedy. Be willing to share.

— based on Luke 12:13-21

For Discussion

1. What does it mean to be greedy?

2. What happened to the selfish farmer?

3. Why should we pass on God's blessings to others?

Create • Take • Create • Take • Create • Take • Create • Take • Create

Barn Full O' Hay

A greedy man brings trouble to his family. Proverbs 15:27

What You Need

- patterns from page 78
- construction paper
- scissors
- glue
- markers
- Easter grass
- toothpicks

Before Class

Duplicate the pattern page for each child.

What to Do

1. Have the students cut out the patterns.

2. Instruct the children to trace and cut one barn from red construction paper using the pattern. They should outline the outer edges and cut the doors open on the solid center line.

3. Have the students trace and cut the upper door from construction paper and glue it to the upper front of the barn. They should draw the X on the door with a black marker.

4. Have the children glue the barn on a 9" x 12" sheet of green construction paper. They should glue the barn on the left side of the paper, leaving the doors open.

5. Have the students cut out two lambs from white paper.

6. Demonstrate how to construct a fence from the barn on the edge of the paper using wooden toothpicks. Have the students glue the two lambs in the pasture beyond the fence.

7. Show how to drop a small amount of glue between the barn doors and add Easter grass to represent a barn full of hay.

8. Write or have the students write the memory verse across the top of the page.

77

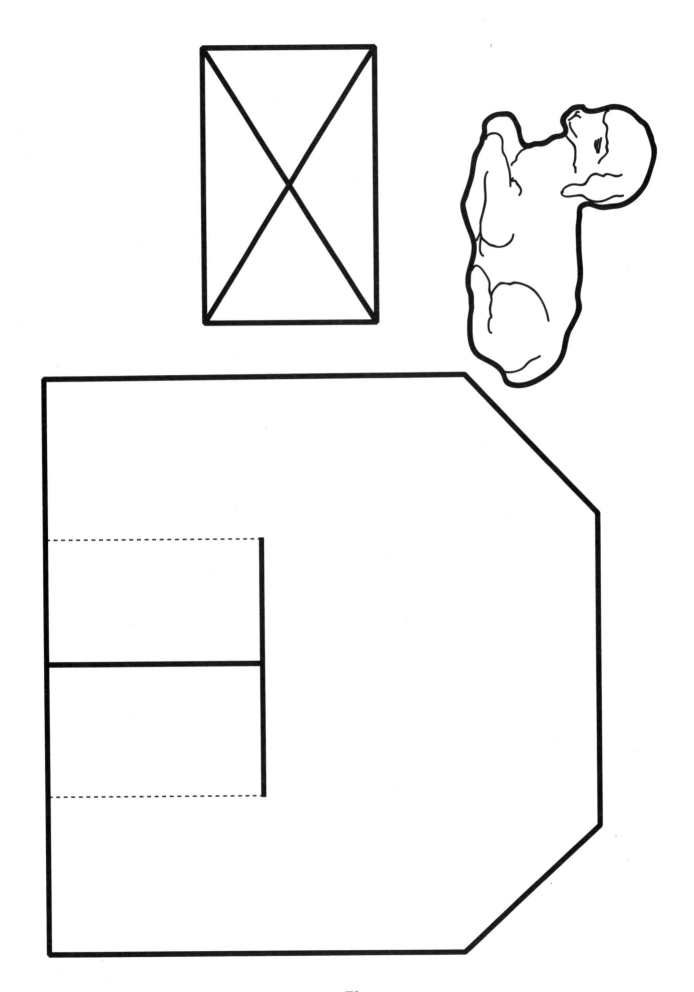

Talents

Ages 5-8

Memory Verse

The righteous still are rewarded.

~Psalm 58:11

....

Rewards

A "reward" is a gift or payment for something you do. Everyone likes to receive rewards. If you want to get rewards, though, you must do good things.

In one of Jesus' parables, a man gave each of his three servants some talents. (In Bible times, a "talent" was money.) Then he went away on a trip. When he returned, he wanted to find out what each of the servants had done with their money. The first two had put their money to work and it had doubled. The master was pleased, so he rewarded them by giving them more money.

The third man, however, had hidden his money and just sat around and waited for his master to return. His master was angry with him for his laziness and took back his talent. Then he threw him out!

God expects us to use what He has given us. He will reward those who work for Him, just as the two men in the parable were rewarded. If we are faithful in the small things, God will give us even greater things. Use your talents wisely for God.

— based on Matthew 25:14-30

For Discussion

1. What is a reward?

2. Name some talents you have.

3. What will happen if you use your talents wisely?

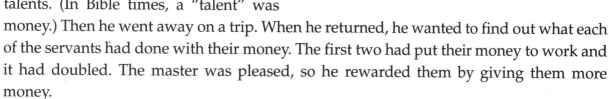

Create • Take • Create • Take • Create • Take • Create • Take • Create

Talented Button Catch Game

What You Need

- toilet tissue tubes
- construction paper
- yarn
- glue
- scissors
- stickers
- buttons
- markers
- stapler

Before Class

Cut construction paper into 4½" x 6" pieces, one per child.

What to Do

1. Have the students write the memory verse in the center of the construction paper rectangle.

2. Show how to wrap the construction paper on a toilet tissue roll and glue it securely.

3. Have the students cut a long length of yarn (approximately 15").

4. Help the students tie a large button to one end of the yarn.

5. Show how to thread the yarn down through the roll and staple it to the back seam.

6. Allow the children to decorate the roll with stickers.

To Play: Hold the roll with one hand. Flip the button up into the air and try to get it through the roll.

The Ten Virgins

Ages 8-11

Memory Verse

Therefore keep watch, because you do not know the day or the hour.

~Matthew 25:13

Be Prepared

To be "prepared" means you are ready and waiting. You have done everything that needs to be done, and you are ready!

Jesus told a story about 10 young ladies who were waiting for the young man they would marry. They all took lamps to go out to meet him. Five ladies were wise because they brought extra oil for their lamps in case they ran out before he got there. Five were foolish because they did not bring any extra oil. They were not prepared. It took a long time for their groom to come and all 10 of the lamps did run out of oil. The five ladies who were prepared filled their lamps and continued to wait. The five foolish ones had to try to buy more oil. While they were away, the bridegroom came and they missed him!

Jesus reminds us that we don't know when He will come back to take us to heaven so we must be prepared. Just like the wise ladies kept oil in the lamps, we need to keep ourselves faithful to God. If we are not prepared, we will miss out.

— based on Matthew 25:1-13

For Discussion

1. What does it mean to be prepared?

2. Who did the five foolish ladies miss by not being prepared?

3. What will we miss if we are not prepared?

Soap Bottle Oil Lamp

What You Need

- plastic dish soap bottles
- scissors
- craft glue
- yarn
- paper towel tubes
- tape
- brown construction paper
- permanent marker
- self-stick labels (optional)

Therefore keep watch, because you do not know the day or the hour.
Matthew 25:13

Before Class

You can pre-cut the bottles if desired.

What to Do

1. Show how to measure two inches from the bottom of the dish soap bottle and draw a circle all the way around it then cut it off.

2. Have the students measure approximately 2½" down from the neck of the bottle, mark it all the way around and cut it off.

3. Have the students pull the tip off the cap. Show how to thread a doubled piece of tan, brown or yellow yarn through the hole (about an inch should be sticking out for a "wick"). Allow the students to pour a small dab of glue inside the cap, then snap the tip back on.

4. Show how to drop a small line of glue just inside the rim of the bottom piece of bottle, then fit the top section down tightly inside the rim. Have the children attach a piece of tape from the neck of the bottle to the bottom on both sides to hold the top and bottom in place while the glue dries. (Remove the tape later.)

5. Meanwhile, have the students cut a 1½" ring from the paper towel roll and cover it with a strip of brown construction paper. They should glue the ring to one end of the lamp for a handle.

6. Have the students write the memory verse on the bottle with a permanent marker or write it on a label and stick it on the front of the lamp.

Two Debtors

Ages 8-11

Memory Verse

Forgive, and you will be forgiven.

~Luke 6:37

. . . .

Forgiveness

Two men owed money to a certain man. One owed him a lot of money, while the other just owed him a little. Neither one had the money to pay back the man, so the man decided to forgive them their debts. That means they didn't have to pay him back.

Jesus asked the disciples which man they thought was the most thankful. They said, "Of course, the one who owed the biggest amount of money."

Jesus told them this: "The one who has been forgiven the most will love the most. In the same way, if you only forgive a little, you will only be loved a little by others."

Be generous with your forgiveness and blessings will come back to you!

— based on Luke 7:40-50

For Discussion

1. What is a debt?

2. Who was most thankful for the man's decision and why?

3. How can we be generous with our forgiveness?

Create • Take • Create • Take • Create • Take • Create • Take • Create

Barking Bank

What You Need

- dog patterns from page 85
- empty powdered drink containers
- scissors
- black markers
- wiggle eyes
- brown construction paper
- craft foam
- craft glue
- small black pom-poms
- yarn

Before Class

Duplicate the dog patterns from page 85 for each child.

What to Do

1. Have the students cover the outside of a powdered drink container by gluing a 4¼" x 9¼" piece of brown construction paper to the container.

2. Help the children cut a slot in the cover for coins.

3. Have the children cut out the patterns and use them to cut and trace the pieces from craft foam using any color they choose.

4. Assemble the head as shown using a black pom-pom for the nose and wiggle eyes. The students should draw in the details of the face, feet and paws with a black marker.

5. Have the children glue the feet to the front bottom of the bank first. Do the gluing in steps, allowing time to hold the parts in place for a few minutes of drying time.

6. Have the students glue the paws to the upper front of the bank.

7. Show how to glue the head to the rim of the lid so that the lid can be easily removed for taking out coins. After gluing the head, help the students tightly tie a string of yarn across the face and around the lid to hold it in place while drying.

8. Have the students glue the tail on the back.

9. Instruct the children to write the memory verse on the side.

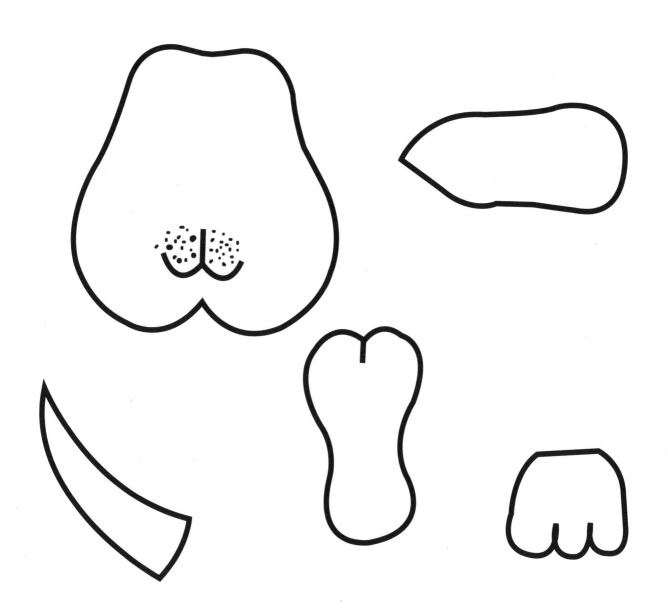

Two Masters

Ages 8-11

Memory Verse

Choose for yourselves this day whom you will serve.

~Joshua 24:15

Service

Have you ever tried to work for two different people at the same time? It is very hard to do. In fact, you will probably end up in trouble with one of them.

In Luke, Jesus said that a person cannot serve two masters at the same time. He said you will end up loving one master and hating the other.

When we talk of a master, it doesn't have to be a specific person. It can be a thing, like money. If we devote our whole lives to making money, it becomes our master. Everything we do will revolve around it. It is what we live for!

We must make the choice of who our master will be and then serve him wholeheartedly. When you choose to serve the Lord, you have chosen the best Master.

— based on Luke 16:1-15

For Discussion

1. Why is it hard to work for two masters?

2. Name some "things" that can be a master.

3. Who is the Master we should serve, and why?

Create • Take • Create • Take • Create • Take • Create • Take • Create

Coin Match Game

What You Need

- patterns from pages 88 and 89
- scissors
- glue
- markers
- construction paper
- clear, self-stick plastic
- poster board
- stapler

Before Class

Duplicate the patterns for each child. Cut construction paper into 8" x 8" squares, two per child.

What to Do

1. Have the students color the coins as appropriately as possible. They should outline the number cards with bright-colored markers.

2. Instruct the students to glue both sheets to thin poster board. Assist them as they cover the sheets with clear, self-stick plastic.

3. Have the students cut the sheets into cards.

4. Show how to make two simple "wallets" by folding an 8" x 8" square of construction paper in half and stapling each end. Then fold them in the middle.

5. Have the students write the memory verse on each wallet.

<u>To Play the Game:</u>

Mix the "coin" cards and lay them face down on one side of the table.

Mix the money amount cards and lay them face down on the other side of the table.

Player one turns over a coin card, decides how much money it represents and then picks an amount card that he or she believes will be the same amount in coins.

If the player is correct, he or she puts the match in a wallet. That player can then take a second turn. If he or she is incorrect, the player must turn both cards back over and go on to player two.

The game continues until all matches have been made.

8¢	15¢	20¢	30¢
12¢	7¢	55¢	25¢
35¢	75¢	50¢	40¢

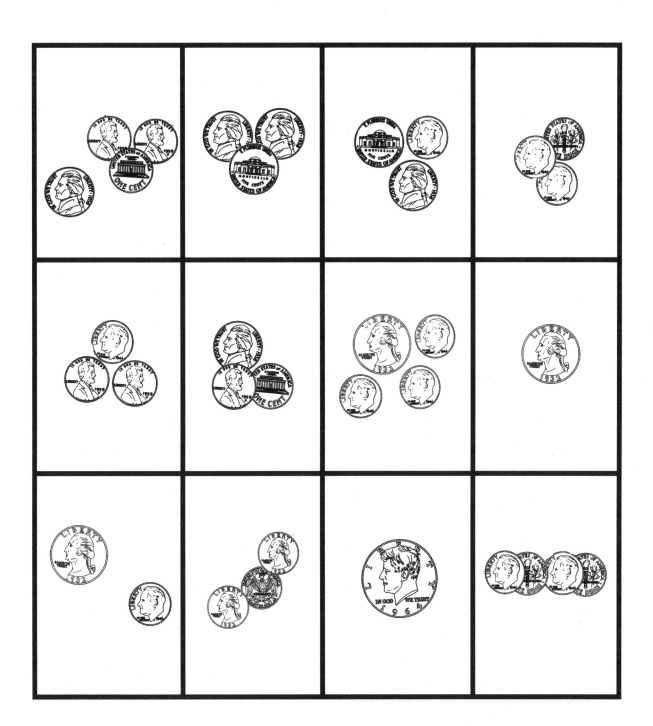

Widow's Offering

Ages 5-8

Memory Verse

God loves a cheerful giver.

~2 Corinthians 9:7

....

Giving

One day Jesus was sitting in the temple observing people as they came to worship. Many rich people came and put large amounts of money in the offering box. Then a widow came by and put in two pennies.

Jesus used this as an example from which to teach. He told the people that she had given more than any of the others that day. The rich people had a lot to give, but they only gave a small part of what they had. The widow had very little and gave it all. Her gift was greater.

We are reminded many times in the Bible to be givers, not just of money but of time, talents and other things. We should not give to get something in return, but because God tells us to. He will bless a willing giver.

— based on Mark 12:41-44

For Discussion

1. How much money did the widow give?

2. Why did Jesus say it was greater than the other offerings?

3. What can we give Jesus besides money?

Create • Take • Create • Take • Create • Take • Create • Take • Create

Pretty Penny Purse

What You Need

- purse pattern from page 92
- craft foam
- yarn
- scissors
- paper punch
- markers

Before Class

God loves a cheerful giver.

2 Cor. 9:7

Duplicate the purse pattern for each child. Cut a 48" length of yarn for each child. If craft foam is unavailable, use felt, lightweight poster board or construction paper.

What to Do

1. Let each child use the pattern to trace and cut one purse from craft foam.

2. Go around and cut the slit on the lower flap of each child's foam.

3. Show how to punch holes along the sides as indicated.

4. Give each student a length of yarn and have them fold it to double (about 24").

5. Show how to fold the flap up and line up the holes. Have the students begin lacing the purse from the bottom right. They should continue upward, leaving a length of yarn about 9" across the top for a handle before starting down the opposite side. Help them tie off the ends.

6. Show how to insert the top tab into the slit. Write or have the students write the memory verse on the back of the purse with a marker.

Create • Take • Create • Take • Create • Take • Create • Take • Create

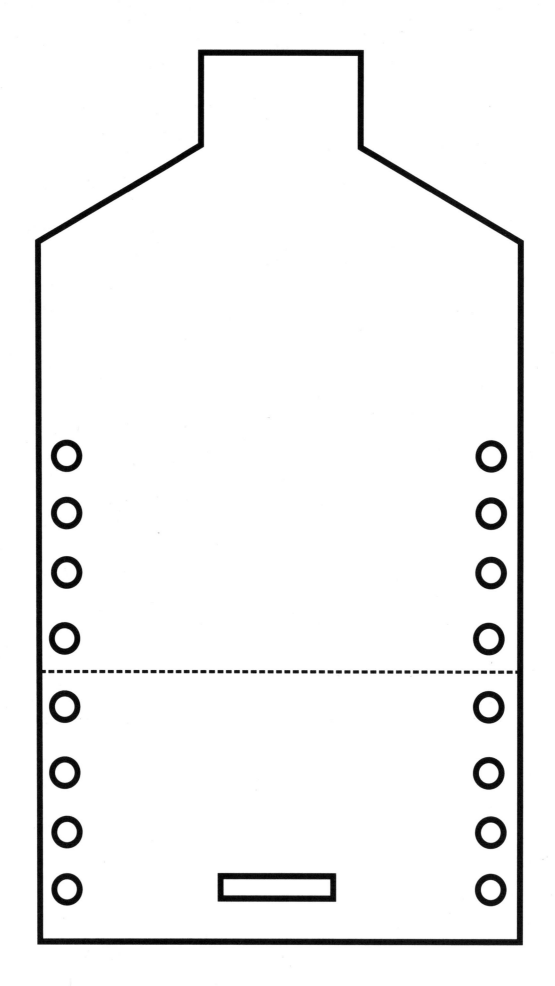